Presenting Princess Ladybug

Princess Ladybug

Written and Illustrated by
Pancheta Barnett

Order this book online at www.trafford.com
or email orders@trafford.com

Most Trafford titles are also available at major online book retailers.

Trafford
PUBLISHING® www.trafford.com
North America & international
toll-free: 844 688 6899 (USA & Canada)
fax: 812 355 4082

Our mission is to efficiently provide the world's finest, most comprehensive book publishing service, enabling every author to experience success. To find out how to publish your book, your way, and have it available worldwide, visit us online at www.trafford.com

Because of the dynamic nature of the Internet, any web addresses or links contained in this book may have changed since publication and may no longer be valid. The views expressed in this work are solely those of the author and do not necessarily reflect the views of the publisher, and the publisher hereby disclaims any responsibility for them.

Any people depicted in stock imagery provided by Getty Images are models, and such images are being used for illustrative purposes only.
Certain stock imagery © Getty Images.

ISBN: 978-1-6987-0908-6 (sc)
978-1-6987-0907-9 (e)

Library of Congress Control Number: 2021916317

Print information available on the last page.

Trafford rev. 03/16/2022

Presenting Princess Ladybug

This book is dedicated to
my daughter **Rhonda**
and to everyone in the world
who loves and collects
Ladybugs.

Presenting Princess Ladybug

This Book Belongs to

_____

Presenting Princess Ladybug
Table of Contents

Presenting Princess Ladybug

who has 2 antennae

6 legs

6 black dots on her red coat…

Princess Ladybug

is carnivorous and loves to eat
lots of aphids, mites and scales...

Princess Ladybug

is happiest when she is with her three best friends...

Princess Ladybug's

three best friends' names are:
Daun, Phidy and Sumer...

Princess Ladybug

and her three best friends
Daun, Phidy and Sumer
dance together...

Princess Ladybug

and her three best friends
huddle together in winter...

Princess Ladybug

and her three best friends awake
in the Spring…
The beginning…

Some Facts About Ladybugs

Ladybugs are also called Ladybird Beetles.

Thousands of years ago the ladybug beetle, once considered holy, was dedicated to the Virgin Mary and was called "Beetle of our Lady". Some say it is good luck to see a ladybug.

Ladybugs have six short legs, two antennae and usually have brightly coloured wings with black dots. Ladybugs can be red, orange, blue, yellow and (the head-less) brown in colour with black spots or they can also be black with red spots. Ladybugs can have zero to more than thirteen dots (six patterned spots on each wing and one shared spot). Ladybugs wear their skeletal frame (their wings) outwards, outside their bodies.

Millions of ladybugs are produced each summer. Larvae can be found wherever there are aphids. The ladybug life cycle is about 4 weeks. Large groups of ladybug beetles hibernate together each winter at the same location.

Farmers and gardeners love ladybugs and buy them in large quantities. Then they use them to control insect pests such as aphids, mites and scales from destroying our fruits and vegetables.

Some ladybugs are carnivorous and some are vegetarians feeding on plants and potatoes which are destructive. Two of these are the Squash Beetle and the Mexican Bean Beetle.

Please do not harm ladybugs. If you find them, let them go gently on their way. Also do not use pesticide on them. Ladybugs are very important to the environment and humanity. Ants and spiders love to feast on ladybugs.

The name 'ladybug' is used for both female and male.

Presenting Princess Ladybug

Written and Illustrated by Pancheta Barnett Ph.D., Hon.

About the Author

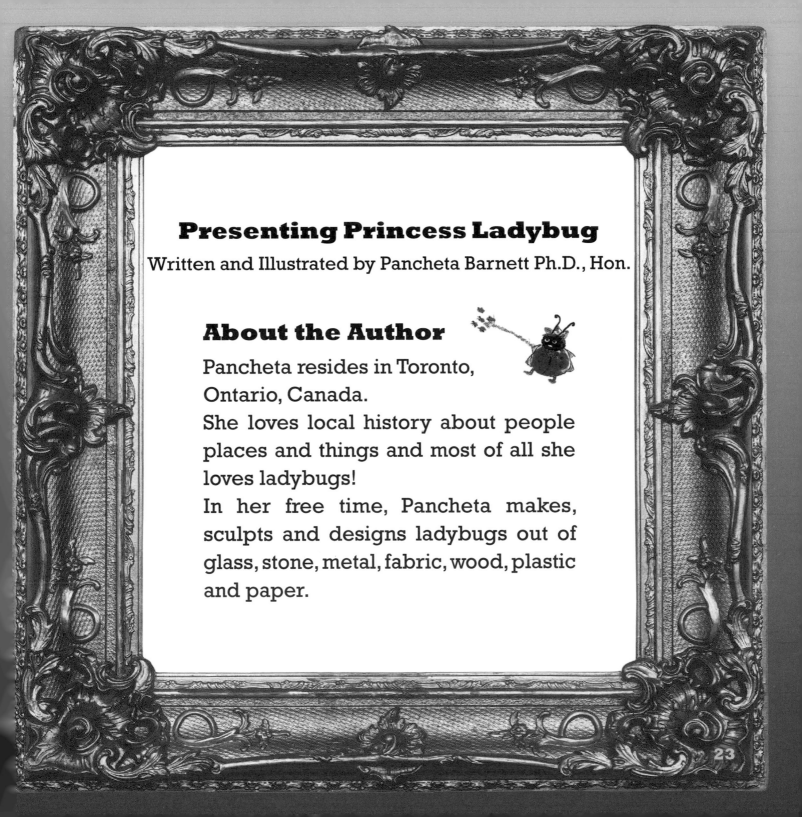

Pancheta resides in Toronto, Ontario, Canada.

She loves local history about people places and things and most of all she loves ladybugs!

In her free time, Pancheta makes, sculpts and designs ladybugs out of glass, stone, metal, fabric, wood, plastic and paper.

Printed in the United States
by Baker & Taylor Publisher Services